Diwali

Lori Dittmer

seedlings

CREATIVE EDUCATION • CREATIVE PAPERBACKS

Published by Creative Education and Creative Paperbacks
P.O. Box 227, Mankato, Minnesota 56002
Creative Education and Creative Paperbacks
are imprints of The Creative Company
www.thecreativecompany.us

Design by Ellen Huber; production by Colin O'Dea
Art direction by Rita Marshall
Printed in China

Photographs by Alamy (Tim Gainey), Getty Images (Abhishek Dwivedi/EyeEm, gulfu photography/Moment, Suman S Rao/EyeEm), iStockphoto (ajaykampani, anshu18, byheaven, ePhotocorp, Naypong, phive2015, PRASANNAPIX, RapidEye, Arundhati Sathe, SoumenNath, spukkato, svrid79, wedninth), Shutterstock (phive, StockImageFactory.com)

Library of Congress Cataloging-in-Publication Data
Names: Dittmer, Lori, author.
Title: Diwali / Lori Dittmer.
Series: Seedlings.
Includes index.
Summary: A kindergarten-level introduction to Diwali, covering the holiday's history, popular traditions, and such defining symbols as clay lamps and rangoli designs.
Identifiers: LCCN 2019053289 / ISBN 978-1-64026-327-7 (hardcover) / ISBN 978-1-62832-859-2 (pbk) / ISBN 978-1-64000-457-3 (eBook)
Subjects: LCSH: Divali—Juvenile literature.
Classification: LCC BL1239.82.D58 D57 2020 / DDC 294.5/36—dc23

CCSS: RI.K.1, 2, 3, 4, 5, 6, 7; RI.1.1, 2, 3, 4, 5, 6, 7; RF.K.1, 3; RF.1.1

First Edition HC 9 8 7 6 5 4 3 2 1
First Edition PBK 9 8 7 6 5 4 3 2 1

TABLE OF CONTENTS

Hello, Diwali! **4**

When Is Diwali? **6**

Holiday Symbols **8**

Good over Evil **11**

Goddess of Wealth **13**

Holiday Food **14**

How Do People Celebrate? **16**

Goodbye, Diwali! **18**

Picture Diwali **20**

Words to Know **22**

Read More **23**

Websites **23**

Index **24**

Hello, Diwali!

Diwali is a festival. People who are not Hindu celebrate it, too.

Diwali is in October or November. It usually lasts five days.

Lights shine from clay lamps.

Colorful shapes are made on floors. These are called *rangoli*.

Diwali is about good winning over evil. Once, a prince freed his wife from a bad king. The people lit lamps to welcome them home.

Diwali also honors the goddess of wealth. Her name is Lakshmi.

People share many sweet treats.

Families eat large meals together.

People pray together.
They light sparklers.

They dress in new clothes.

Goodbye,

Diwali!

Picture Diwali

 lamp

 rangoli

sweets

Lakshmi

goddess: a female god

Hindu: relating to Hindus, people whose religion is Hinduism; it is widely practiced in South Asia

pray: to communicate with God or gods

Read More

Bentley, Joyce. *Happy Divali.*
London: Wayland, 2016.

Grack, Rachel. *Diwali.*
Minneapolis: Bellwether Media, 2017.

Websites

DKfindout: Diwali
https://www.dkfindout.com/us/more-find-out/festivals-and
-holidays/diwali/
Read more about Diwali.

YouTube: National Geographic: Diwali – Festival of Lights
https://www.youtube.com/watch?v=HrrW3rO51ak
Watch a video to see how people celebrate this holiday.

Index

families 15
food 14, 15
Hinduism 6, 13
history 11
Lakshmi 13
symbols 8, 9, 11
timing 7
traditions 16, 17